New York City
a Photographic Portrait

New York City
a Photographic Portrait

170 PRINTS BY

VICTOR LAREDO

with captions by THOMAS REILLY

DOVER PUBLICATIONS, INC., NEW YORK

Published in Canada by General Publishing Company, Ltd.,
30 Lesmill Road, Don Mills, Toronto, Ontario.
Published in the United Kingdom by Constable and Company, Ltd., 10 Orange Street, London WC 2.

New York City: a Photographic Portrait is a new work,
first published by Dover Publications, Inc. in 1973. Most of
the photographs were originally published in *New York People
and Places* by Reinhold Publishing Corporation in 1964. The
captions were written especially for the present edition by
Thomas Reilly.

International Standard Book Number: 0-486-22852-5
Library of Congress Catalog Card Number: 72-91058

Manufactured in the United States of America
Dover Publications, Inc.
180 Varick Street
New York, N. Y. 10014

PUBLISHER'S NOTE, 1972

The noted photographer Victor Laredo, who has exhibited at the Museum of Modern Art and the Brooklyn Museum, has been an astute observer of the New York scene for over thirty years. The present album includes 174 examples of his finest work, an arresting personal vision of the island of Manhattan.

Beginning at the Battery, Mr. Laredo guides us steadily northward through the financial district and the City Hall area, into Chinatown, the Lower West Side, the Lower East Side, SoHo, Greenwich Village, the East Village, Chelsea, Gramercy Park, Madison Square, the garment district, Times Square, Rockefeller Center, Park Avenue, the Upper West Side, Central Park, the Upper East Side and Spanish Harlem.

Architecture is of primary importance to Mr. Laredo. Not only does he offer us excellent "portraits" of individual buildings. He also gives us numerous glimpses of delightful ornaments and details that often elude the casual passerby. Above all, there is a wealth of cityscapes, seen from bold and unusual angles, which capture the kaleidoscopically shifting interrelationships of surfaces and contours that compose the real face of Manhattan. The phenomenal rate of urban growth and change is also in evidence here: a number of buildings, including once familiar landmarks, that were photographed by Mr. Laredo less than ten years ago are no more than a memory today.

But the people of New York are also of concern to this photographer. We find them at work: artists and tradesmen, Park Avenue secretaries and members of the city's leading industries, clothing manufacture and printing. We find them at play: in a wide variety of everyday leisure activities, and at public and private festivities. The bustling life of streets and parks is lovingly recorded.

Thomas Reilly's lively captions, compiled from a wide variety of the most recent and reliable source material as well as from painstaking personal investigations, identify the buildings shown and their architectural styles, give detailed histories of many buildings and sites, and offer much information on ethnic lore, the economics of neighborhoods, business statistics and the life of the city in general.

Casual visitor or lifetime resident, on your next walk through New York you will find Mr. Laredo's artistic vision guiding your own eyes toward the unusual view, the telling detail, that you may have overlooked—an enrichment of your experience of the world's most astonishing city.

New York City
a Photographic Portrait

The Staten Island Ferry.

The ferry is still one of the most pleasant ways to sightsee in New York and is undoubtedly the least expensive. At 5¢ a ride, it works out to about a penny a mile.

Castle Clinton in Battery Park.

Built as the West Battery by John McComb, architect of New York's City Hall, in 1808-1811, this structure and its twin, the East Battery (Castle Williams on Governor's Island), defended New York Harbor during the War of 1812. Later roofed-over and renamed Castle Garden, it became a music-hall and the scene of Jenny Lind's first American concert in 1850. Still later it was re-modeled by the architectural firm of McKim, Mead and White to serve as the New York Aquarium from 1896 to 1941. Since 1946, it has been designated a National Historic Monument. Fog-shrouded buildings in the financial district loom in the background.

(Opposite) Skyscrapers in downtown Manhattan.

Gleaming against the dramatic backdrop provided by a storm over New York Harbor, these towers of industry and government look like the fantastic battlements of a fairy-tale city. At the left is the Singer Building, a Beaux-Arts landmark by Ernest Flagg, erected in 1908 and demolished in 1967. The building just left of center is the Roman Eclectic Municipal Building by McKim, Mead and White, 1914. The two towers on the right are by Cass Gilbert. The building with the gold pyramid is the U. S. Court House in Foley Square, 1936; the other is that Gothic cathedral of commerce, the Woolworth Building, 1913.

Bowling Green.

The small park for which this section of the financial district is named was formalized in 1732, and is thus the oldest established park in the city. The building at the right is the U. S. Customs House, designed in 1907 by Cass Gilbert, with monumental sculptures symbolizing the four continents by Daniel Chester French. Behind it is 2 Broadway, 1959, Emery Roth and Sons.

(Opposite) On Nassau St., looking toward the intersection of Wall and Broad Sts.

The building at the left is the Federal Hall National Memorial, the most superb example of Greek Revival architecture in New York. A simplified version of the Parthenon, it was built as a customs house in 1842 by Town and Davis with John Frazee. The name Federal Hall actually refers to an earlier building on the same site which served as the scene of Washington's inauguration. On the right, the temple-façade of the New York Stock Exchange, a product of the later classical revival which followed the Columbian Exposition of 1893. The Exchange was designed by George B. Post in 1903; its workings can be observed by visitors on free guided tours.

Delmonico's Restaurant (now Oscar's Delmonico), 56 Beaver St., at William St.

The Delmonico's restaurants were at the height of their popularity when James Brown Lord designed this building in 1891. It is a rarity among American restaurants in that it was designed and built specifically to enhance the experience of dining out, rather than installed in a store-front as an afterthought. Even today, this lovely edifice still manages to maintain much of the elegance of its era.

Lower Manhattan from Brooklyn Heights in the late Sixties.

The 1960 construction of the Chase Manhattan Bank Building (Skidmore, Owings and Merrill, fourth tower from left in this photo) started a building boom which has effected dramatic changes in the Wall St. area in the few years since this photo was taken. Among these have been the demolition of the Singer Building, on the right, and the construction of dozens of sleek new skyscrapers including the twin towers of the World Trade Center. When this picture was taken, the skyline was still dominated by the office towers of the Twenties and Thirties. The three tallest here are, left to right: The First National City Trust Company Building, 1931, Cross and Cross; 40 Wall St., 1929, H. Craig Severance and Yasuo Matsui; and 60 Wall Tower, 1932, Clinton and Russell. The nativity scene on the Brooklyn piers in the foreground was formerly erected annually at Christmas by the men of the International Longshoremen's Association, but the custom has since been discontinued.

The Potter Building, Beekman and Nassau Sts.

The Potter Building was New York's first introduction to the illimitable ornamental possibilities of terra cotta, a material which soon became all-too-popular. Designed by N. Y. Starkweather and built in 1883, it was one of the first buildings in this city to use structural steel. Today, in spite of the zany exuberance of its decoration, the strong vertical lines of its facade express the idea of a skyscraper as meaningfully as the ziggurat outline of the newer building across City Hall Park.

The Tribune Building, Printing House Square,
Park Row and Spruce St.

This building stood to the immediate southeast of City Hall. It was designed by Richard Morris Hunt in a short-lived Beaux-Arts style known as Neo-Grec, which attempted to simplify the Greek orders of ornament to suit the demands of modern construction techniques. When this building was put up in 1873, it was the first of the elevator office buildings. Demolished in the mid-Sixties, its site is now occupied by Pace College and new approaches to the Brooklyn Bridge.

Beekman St. from Gold St. to Pearl St.

Everything shown in this photograph, including the roadway itself, has disappeared; and the area has become the superblock site of a large apartment complex. The bright white building toward the end of the block is the subject of the photo on the next page.

Nassau and Fulton Sts., in the heart of the financial district.
The building on the far corner is the Bennett Building, Arthur Gilman, 1873.

(Opposite) 84 Beekman St.,
the St. George Building.

This fanciful loft building stood on Beekman St. at Cliff St. It was probably built during the 1860's or 70's, when a vogue for the mansard roofs of Paris's Second Empire swept the United States. As the confusion of classical orders and the profuse decoration indicate, this was a period when no coherent architectural style predominated, and peculiar but charming buildings like this one were appearing everywhere. Nor were the owners of this building alone in putting on airs. The sign on the gate announces that the alley which gave access to the Scheiren Leather Goods Building in the background is called "Chapel Court."

Chambers St., looking east toward
the Municipal Building.

By 1914, New York City was paying the staggering sum of $509,420 annually in office space rentals for its departments, and the construction of the Municipal Building was undertaken as an economy move. The space gained was quickly filled, of course, and today it seems that the city rents space in every building in the City Hall area. At any rate, the city fathers chose this site, two triangular plots on either side of Chambers St., which more or less demanded a building with a road running through it. McKim, Mead and White won the design competition which followed with this Roman classical monument to city government, although some of the other entries were a good deal more ingenious in straddling Chambers St. At the top, "Civic Virtue" by Adolph A. Weinman stares west toward the Hudson River and New Jersey. One of the city's best views of the Brooklyn Bridge is available free from the Reference and Research Center on the 22nd floor.

Chinatown.

Only a few short blocks from Foley Square, the bureaucratic center of the city, everything suddenly becomes Chinese: food, magazines, even movies. It is wonderful to realize that so thoroughly exotic a neighborhood can thrive in a modern American city.

Cardinal Hayes Place.

This quiet little street skirts the back of the United States Court House, just around the corner from the agitation of Foley Square.

Mott St., Chinatown.

(Opposite) Broadway and Leonard St., looking southeast toward the Municipal Building.

The building at the left is 346 Broadway, built by Griffith Thomas in 1870, and later remodeled in Italian Renaissance style by McKim, Mead and White. This was originally the home office of the New York Life Insurance Company whose monogram (NYLICo) can be discerned in the medallions of the decorative cornice.

Thomas and Church Sts.

In the 1850's and 1860's, thousands of cast-iron façades arose in the commercial districts of Manhattan. The popularity of cast iron was due to the fact that it allowed the economical reproduction of elaborate detail work, previously possible only in carved stone, in an era when architectural detail remained an important element of design. The development of processes for the mass-production of more versatile structural steel elements brought an end to this era. This building, 54 Worth St., was designed by William Field and Sons in about 1860. It was demolished several years ago.

Broadway and Thomas St.

Two of the handsomest buildings in New York's southern cast-iron district (between Broadway and West Broadway from Canal to Duane Sts.) are these twins at 317 and 319 Broadway. Built in 1865, they have been proposed for landmark designation. Unfortunately, the kind of unsympathetic alterations the first and second floors of these buildings have received is not at all unusual in this area.

Broadway and Franklin St.

361-363 Broadway, formerly the James S. White Building, was designed by W. Wheeler Smith and built in 1882. Note the splendidly decorative treatment of the cast-iron columns.

131-133 Duane St. (at Church St.)

Hudson and Thomas Sts., looking south toward Duane Park.

The pedestal of the flagstaff in the park bears this inscription:

Duane Park is the last remnant of greensward of the "Annetje Jans Farm," granted in 1636 by Governor Wouter Van Twiller to Roeloff and Annetje Jans. After the death of Roeloff Jans, his widow married the Reverend Everadus Bogardus, second minister of the Dutch Church of New Amsterdam and the farm became known as The Dominie's Bouwerie.—In 1670, it was sold to the English Governor Sir Francis Lovelace, but was later confiscated by the Duke of York and deeded in 1705 to Trinity Church. This triangle was purchased from Trinity Church by the City of New York in 1795 for the sum of five dollars as a park for the public.—Reconstructed in 1940.

(Opposite) The Washington Market area.

The following five photographs depict a section of the lower west side of Manhattan which was, until recently, one of the architecturally most interesting districts in the city. By and large, new construction in this area ceased around the turn of the century, and a great many of the buildings which, in these photos, serve as markets and warehouses began as townhouses in pre-Civil War New York. A number of the buildings on the corner of Harrison and Washington Sts., for example, were designed about 1800 by John McComb as townhouses for himself and his friends. In this district too, James Bogardus erected the first of his cast-iron buildings in 1848, on the corner of Murray and Washington Sts. Shortly after these pictures were taken, however, clearing began for the Washington Market Urban Renewal Project. Already, everything west of Greenwich St. and south of Beach St. has been razed for a project which will eventually provide housing, schools, and commercial space. This development will undoubtedly prove an exciting addition to lower Manhattan and will, fortunately, provide for the preservation of some of the more distinguished structures in the area, but the demolition of such a comprehensive collection of 19th-century buildings is an irrevocable loss to the city. This photo, for example, shows the intersection of Washington and Reade Sts.; and every building shown here has since been demolished.

Greenwich and Harrison Sts., northeast corner.
This red-brick oddity with its pseudo-classical swags, pilasters, and pediments is still standing, and still has its window sills crowded with flower pots.

Harrison St., looking west toward Greenwich St.
Everything beyond Greenwich St. is now torn down. The building partly hidden by the column at the right is the subject of the photo above.

Reade St., looking east from Greenwich St.

Here, at least, nothing has been ripped down—yet. Reade St. contains a number of early 19th-century structures and, in many cases, the latest "renovations" occurred during the cast-iron era of the 1860's. The pyramid just visible over the roof-tops at the end of the street is the top of the United States Court House in Foley Square.

(Opposite above) Harrison St., looking east toward Washington St.

The small houses with dormers on Washington St. and on the corner of Harrison and Washington are Federal townhouses designed by friends of John McComb over a period from 1797 to 1828. The house McComb designed for himself, 315-317 Washington St. is outside the photo to the right. Shown here are, far right, 327, 329 and 331 Washington St. and, on the corner, 29, 31 and 33 Harrison St. The Washington Market plan calls for the preservation of these houses and they will hopefully be restored to serve as homes within the complex.

(Opposite below) Greenwich St., looking south from Chambers St.

The buildings along the east side of Greenwich St. still stand but they are boarded up and apparently slated for demolition. The glimpse afforded here of the tops of the Chase Manhattan Building and 40 Wall St. has since been cut off by new construction in the Wall St. area.

Romanesque Revival in a tenement setting, at 7 Elizabeth St.

(Opposite) 49 Elizabeth St.

Throughout the 19th century, American architects were preoccupied with the question of which architectural styles best suited which building uses. Romanesque Revival was the favorite for commercial structures from about 1845 up through the 90's, and this is a rather good late example.

A Gypsy party on the Lower East Side.

Historically, the Lower East Side has served as the first American home of the various immigrant groups as they arrived in New York. As this and the following seven photos show, it is still an area of exciting ethnic variety.

A Turkish dancer in a cafe on Allen St.

A Matzo bakery in Rivington St.

Herring vendors, Lower East Side.

Katz's Deli, E. Houston St.

Storefront shrine on Mulberry St.

Little Italy, which extends from Canal to Houston Sts. and from Lafayette St. to the Bowery, is now populated mostly by older people, as the younger Italian-Americans abandon Manhattan for the suburbs. Twice a year during the street-festivals, however, this area becomes the focus of attention and everyone in New York becomes an Italian for a few days.

(Opposite) Mulberry St. during the Festival of San Gennaro.

There are two major street festivals held in Little Italy annually. The Feast of San Antonio is celebrated on Sullivan St. during the week of June 13th; the Feast of San Gennaro on Mulberry St. the week of September 19th. The attractions include a great variety of Italian foods, games of chance for the benefit of the Church, and a chance to shake hands with the mayor if he happens to be up for re-election.

Artist's studio in SoHo.

New York has long held a position as a center of innovation in the arts. The prestige the city's artists bring New York does pay a real, if somewhat hard to calculate, annual monetary return; but the facts of life in the real-estate business seem pitted against the artists. The cycle runs like this: seeking large working spaces for low rents, impoverished artists move into run-down and slum areas of the city; the areas they settle acquire reputations as arts' centers and become fashionable; the areas become popular, rents rise, and the artists are driven elsewhere. This has already happened in Greenwich Village and the process is now going on in the Chelsea area. One of the newer artist colonies is in an area west of Little Italy now called SoHo (for *South of Houston* St.). At present, its thoroughly dilapidated buildings seem safe from the encroachments of fashion, but real-estate agents are already hiking rents for "gallery space" in what were, five years ago, unrentable loft properties.

(Opposite) Mulberry St., shrine of San Gennaro.

San Gennaro (Saint Januarius) was an early Christian bishop and martyr, and is the patron saint of Naples. The September festival celebrates the tradition that, at this time of year, reliquary phials of the saint's blood are exhibited to the faithful in Naples whereupon the blood miraculously liquifies.

Greene and Grand Sts.

These buildings are in New York's northern cast-iron district (Canal to Houston Sts., between Broadway and West Broadway). The building at the right is 90-94 Grand St. The building at the left is 80-88 Grand St., built in 1881 by Robert Mook.

468 West Broadway.

Puck Building.

Although *Puck* ceased publication one year after its purchase by William Randolph Hearst in 1917, the chubby figure of Puck himself survives here and on the masthead of the Hearst Sunday comic supplement, where he appears with his familiar jibe: "What fools these mortals be."

(Opposite) Puck Building, Lafayette St., between Houston and Jersey Sts.

From 1877 to 1918, one of New York's most popular journals was the humor weekly *Puck*. Its founder, first editor, and chief illustrator was Joseph Keppler, who is said to have introduced the German art of caricature into American journalism. *Puck's* special forte was satire, and, under the vigorous leadership of such editors as Keppler and H. C. Bunner, it consistently attacked political corruption and social injustice. This interesting Romanesque Revival building was designed by Albert Wagner and built in 1885.

Washington Square Village, Bleecker St. and West Broadway.

Designed by S. J. Kessler, these buildings were completed in 1958 and are owned by New York University. It seems that the noisier and dirtier the city gets, the faster these little patios appear. To *have* one, of course, is a status symbol; but it is as rare to see anyone *using* one as it is to see a new apartment building without them.

Demolition on E. 9th St.
A familiar scene in Greenwich Village: small buildings are destroyed to make room for nondescript high-rises like the one in the background.

526 West Broadway.

A small storefront imaginatively converted into a small apartment building directly across the street from Washington Square Village.

St. Luke's Place, Greenwich Village.

The ginkgo trees, beautifully proportioned private homes, and quiet
Federal detailing make this one of the most splendid residential
blocks in the city. Pictured here is the entrance to No. 6, for a
time the home of New York's flamboyant mayor from 1926 to 1932,
James J. ("Gentleman Jimmy") Walker.

This small garage (at 49-51 Downing St.) was once, of course, a stable.

13 Morton St.
A sampling of the oddities of architectural detailing to be found on the sidestreets of Greenwich Village.

West Greenwich Village.

137 W. 10th St.

W. 4th St., Greenwich Village.

Washington Arch, Washington Square Park, Greenwich Village.

The first Washington Arch was a temporary wooden structure which spanned Fifth Avenue somewhat north of the square. Designed by McKim, Mead and White and erected in 1889 to commemorate the centennial of Washington's inauguration, it created such a sensation that the public clamored for a permanent model. Accordingly, a committee was formed, funds were solicited, and the marble arch was dedicated in 1892. The sculpture on the left, "Washington in War," is by Herman A. MacNeil. On the right, "Washington in Peace," by Alexander Calder's father, Alexander Stirling Calder. To the right of the arch, the tower of the Judson Memorial Church, 1892, also designed by McKim, Mead and White, in the style of the Italian Renaissance.

Around the fountain, Washington Square Park.

Fifth Avenue traffic used to run right through the park but, thanks to public pressure, it has been closed to vehicular traffic since 1964. Unfortunately, in the recently completed renovation, the city fathers have seen fit to replace the asphalt paving with brick paving rather than try to re-introduce greenery into the park's central area.

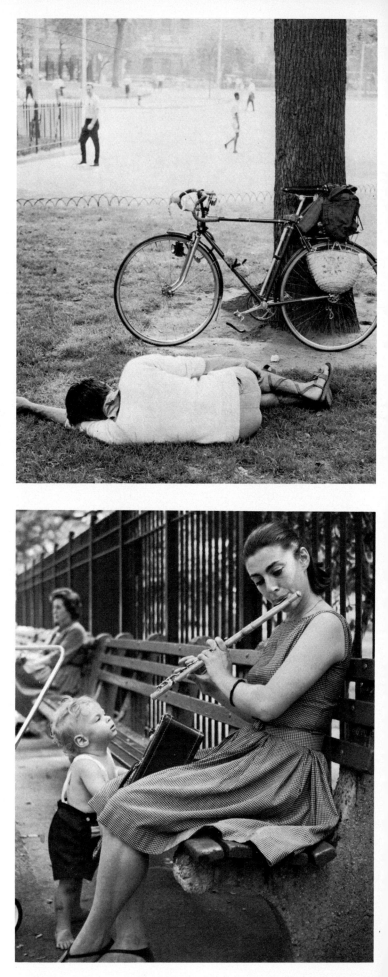

Views of Washington Square Park.

Around Washington Square Park.
The Washington Square Outdoor Art Show is held twice each year from late May through June and again from late August through September.

No. 12 Washington Square North.

A doorway on "The Row," which used to run all along Washington Square North. The original houses (Nos. 21-26) were built in 1831 and are attributed to Town and Davis, New York's leading Greek Revival architects. No. 12 was probably built around 1833. In the late 1930's, the original houses from No. 7 to No. 13 were demolished and a small apartment building was erected. The original façades were re-erected as false fronts incorporated into the new building.

No. 6 Washington Square North.

This fine old building, dating from about 1833, remains in close to original condition.

60 W. 9th St.

Lower Fifth Avenue, near Washington Square.

Newel post at 30 W. 10th St.

No. 30 is one of the row houses in the "English Terrace" Row (20-40 W. 10th St.), built 1855-1856.

Cast iron at 21 W. 11th St.

Newel post at 32 W. 10th St.

Another house in the elegant "English Terrace" Row.

Carved teakwood at 7 E. 10th St.

This ornate woodwork was commissioned in India   the behest of its owner, Ardsley Van Arsdale.
by Lockwood de Forest expressly for this house at

21 W. 11th St.

This 19th-century townhouse with Victorian trimmings stands almost directly opposite the site of No. 18 W. 11th St., which was destroyed in a catastrophic explosion with political overtones in 1970.

Hotel van Rensselaer, 15 E. 11th St.

This building is typical of the cozy, "smart" hotels that enjoyed a great vogue up through the early part of this century. Today, largely superseded by the newer and bigger apartment hotels in the Gramercy Park and Central Park West areas, many of these once-charming residences have become dilapidated.

Doorway, Bayard Building.

In a typical attempt to "modernize," the owners of this building have desecrated a classic design, streamlining the lobby and display windows and replacing the original doors. The decorative frame around the main entrance, however, remains as Sullivan designed it.

(Opposite) Bayard Building, 65 Bleeker St., at Crosby St.

Originally the Condict Building, this is the only structure in New York designed by the pioneer modern architect, Louis H. Sullivan. It was built in 1898. The story is that the angels supporting the cornice were reluctantly added by Sullivan at the insistence of the building's owner, Silas Alden Condict.

71-73 Bleecker St.

This is the rear end of the building at 644 Broadway, and it is immediately adjacent to the entrance to the Bayard Building shown in the preceding photograph. The eclecticism of its details, the heaviness of its brownstone arches, and its emphatic rustication provide an illuminating contrast to the coherence of Sullivan's design.

(Opposite) Jones Alley off Bond St.

The building at left is 1-5 Bond St., formerly the Robbins and Appleton Building, a fine example of the Italianate style in cast-iron architecture by S. D. Hatch, 1871.

Grace Church, 800 Broadway.

Designed by James Renwick, Jr. and built in 1846, Grace Church is a magnificent example of Gothic Revival architecture. Renwick later (1858-1879) designed St. Patrick's Cathedral; and, still later, returned to Grace Church to design the building at 806 Broadway (shown here to the left of the church tower) as a Gothic backdrop to the churchyard. The tower to the right of the church tower is the Consolidated Edison Building at Irving Place and 14th St.

Merchants Building, 693 Broadway.
A detail of the frieze at the corner of E. 4th St. and Broadway.

Portico, Cooper Union Foundation Building, Cooper Square.

Built in 1859 by Frederick A. Peterson, Cooper Union is the oldest extant steel-framed building in America, a fact which is not particularly evidenced by the heaviness of its Italianate brownstone façade.

(Opposite) Lafayette St. south of Astor Place.

There are still vantage points in Manhattan from which every building one can see dates from before the turn of the century. Of course, chrome and glass have been added to the storefronts on the ground floor; but, if one doesn't look too closely, blocks like this show what the city must have looked like in the Nineties. At the left is Colonnade Row, built as a complex of expensive private homes in 1836, but now degraded to a variety of commercial uses. This may well be the most elegant group of buildings ever erected in New York, but it has not received the respect or attention it properly deserves. Only four of the original nine houses remain, the rest have been unceremoniously demolished. Where there are now twelve slender Corinthian columns, there once were twenty-eight.

13 St. Mark's Place.

The East Village begins at Astor Place and here, along St. Mark's Place between Astor Place and Second Avenue, it is a pleasant place with wide sidewalks and small shops. Farther east, the rents are lower and the environment is seedier, and the avenues east of Tompkins Square Park remain virtual slums.

E. 10th St. between First and Second Aves.

(Opposite) 213 and 215 E. 10th St.

The Michelangelesque reclining figures on these tenement façades must have been standardized commercial sculptural elements, since there are three buildings on this block alone which employ them.

Ornamental panel, St. Mark's Place, between First Ave. and Ave. A.

Ornamental panel, St. Mark's Place, between First and Second Aves.

Apartment building on St. Mark's Place at Ave. A.

71

Newel post on 11th St.,
between Third and Fourth Aves.

Newel post on St. Mark's Place,
between First Ave. and Ave. A.

E. 8th St., between Aves. B and C.

E. 8th St., between Aves. B and C.

Touch football in Tompkins Square Park.

Vegetable stand, St. Mark's Place.

Sidewalk flea market, Ave. C.

Bootblack, Avenue C.

The Avenue C Boys Association.

New York is a city of clubs and clubhouses. Among the more prominent are the Metropolitan Club, the Yacht Club, the Harvard Club, the New York Athletic Club, and the Union League, all a bit farther uptown than this humble establishment. The big clubs are certainly richer and grander, but they are far outnumbered by the thousands of neighborhood clubhouses like this spread throughout the city.

Kite Flying on the Lower East Side's Seacoast.

This land has had a more interesting history than its tree-lined sidewalks and baseball diamonds would seem to indicate. In 1636, the land was owned by Jacobus Van Corlaer, the Dutch farmer for whom Corlaer's Hook is named. The waterfront property north of what is now Houston St. remained marshland throughout the 18th century, but New York's thriving shipbuilding industry was already beginning to establish itself here by 1800. In 1807, when Robert Fulton's *Clermont* was built in a shipyard at the foot of Jackson St., this was one of the most important shipbuilding centers on the East Coast. The first steam warship was built here in 1814, and in 1851 the yacht *America* was launched at the foot of 12th St. By 1888, however, the docks had become headquarters for the gangs Jacob Riis photographed in *How the Other Half Lives;* and the New York *Sun* reported that "Decent people are not to be expected here. . . ." By the time the city began construction of the East River Drive in 1935, the waterfront here was all but abandoned. In July, 1936, the City Council authorized acquisition of the area for use as a public park and land-fill and clearing operations began almost immediately.

E. 7th St.

The East Village is another area in which artists have settled in the years since high rents began forcing them to evacuate Greenwich Village.

14th St. from Franklin D. Roosevelt Drive.
The westward vista along 14th St. is here framed by the spare
geometry of Con Edison's East River Power Plant.

S. Klein's, 14th St. and Union Square.

Dance studio, W. 14th St.

Ornamental doorway, 14th St. and Seventh Ave.

8th Ave. at 13th St.

"THE" GREENWICH VILLAGE HUMANE LEAGUE, INC.

Former Siegel-Cooper Department Store, Sixth Ave., between 18th and 19th Sts.

In the last quarter of the 19th century, Sixth Ave. from 18th to 23rd Sts. was the heart of Manhattan's fashionable shopping district; when it was built in 1896, this building's neighbors along the avenue included B. Altman's and Stern Brothers. It was designed by De Lemos and Cordes in the Classical Revival style popularized by the Chicago World's Fair of 1893. The S C monogram is still plainly visible, although the building now houses television production facilities and small business offices.

141-147 Fifth Ave. at 20th St.

19th St. and Irving Place.

13 *Gramercy Park South.*

The Gramercy Park area is one of the most hand-some and gracious in the city. The park itself is private, owned co-operatively by property owners around the square and restricted to residents. Its creation was the result of the imagination of Samuel Ruggles, a New York lawyer, who in 1831 acquired the land as farm acreage and, at great personal expense, converted it into a desirable residential district. Although he realized little profit from the scheme, Ruggles' district flourished and remains today as charmingly successful as he must have envisioned it.

12 Gramercy Park South.

(Left) Madison Square and the Flatiron Building.

The seven acres which now comprise Madison Square Park are all that remain of a 55-block area between Third and Seventh Avenues set aside by the New York Commissioners' Plan of 1811 as a parade ground. In the background of this picture looms the dramatic form of the Flatiron (formerly Fuller) Building, built in 1902 by D. H. Burnam to conform to the triangular plot at the intersection of Fifth Ave. and Broadway. The 22-story Flatiron Building was Fifth Ave.'s first skyscraper and is now designated as a City Landmark.

(Opposite) The Empire State Building at night.

The Chrysler Building's spire appears on the right.

(Below) Midtown skyline and docks along the Hudson River.

The Empire State Building, at left, stands at 34th St. and Fifth Ave. It was built in 1931 by Shreve, Lamb & Harmon. At the right is the Metropolitan Life Tower, at 23rd St. and Madison Ave., 1909, Napoleon LeBrun and Sons. What appear to be twin office buildings on the waterfront in the center of this picture are really ventilation shafts for the Lincoln Tunnel.

Pennsylvania Station, Seventh Ave. and 31st St.

This superlative example of classical revival architecture by McKim, Mead and White was completed in 1910. The inspiration for the design came from the Baths of Caracalla in Rome. Despite vigorous protests, the building was demolished in 1966. It was replaced, in 1968, by the Madison Square Garden Center, consisting of an undistinguished 29-story office tower and the latest Madison Square Garden Arena.

The dismantling of Penn Station.

A pair of the eagles shown above the cornice in this view now flank the Seventh Avenue entrance to the train concourse in the new Madison Square Garden Center.

Seventh Ave. and 38th St., the garment district.

The garment district extends roughly from 30th St. to 39th St. between Sixth and Eighth Aves., with generous spill-overs in all directions. The garment industry's concentration in this section of the city is something of a phenomenon, as the narrow midtown streets make no provision whatsoever for the constant deliveries necessary in this line of business. On weekdays, vehicular congestion in these streets is truly astounding.

The dressmaking industry, hand sewing.

Cutting.

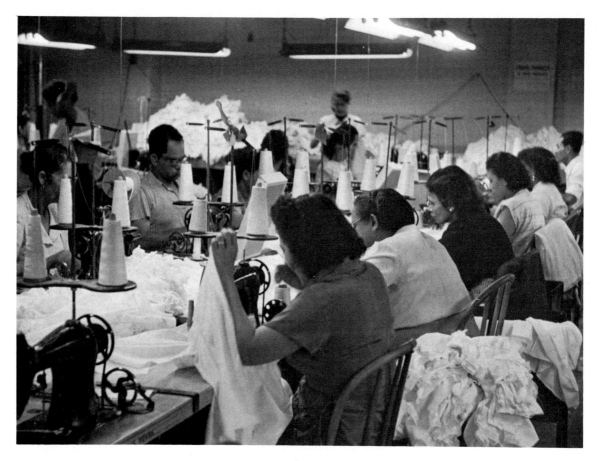

Sewing machine operators.

Machine sewing.

The garment business is New York's largest manufacturing industry with city firms doing over $4 billion business annually in women's wear alone, and employing about 250,000 people.

Haute couture.

The Composing Room, Inc., W. 46th St.

Printing and publishing is New York's second largest industry. The exciting activity shown here is known as reading proof.

Pulling proof.

Broadway and 46th St.

Officially named Duffy Square in honor of Father Duffy, chaplain of New York's "Fighting 69th" Regiment in World War I, this is really merely the northern end of Times Square. There is a statue of Father Duffy in Duffy Square, but the one at right in this view is of showman George M. Cohan.

W. 45th St.

The single block of 45th St. immediately west of Broadway has more theaters than any other street in New York. The quiet elegance of the Music Box Theater's classical facade is seldom noticed amid the neon lights of the theater district.

Along Eighth Ave.

(Opposite)
46th St. east of Broadway.

Grand Central Terminal, Park Ave. and 42nd St.

Time was when nearly all incoming visitors to New York entered the city through the magnificent portals of either Pennsylvania Station or Grand Central Terminal. Penn Station has been destroyed and this noble old building (completed 1913, C. A. Reed and Warren and Wetmore) has had to suffer the installation of tremendous and inappropriate advertising displays. Passing through the main room remains nonetheless an elevating experience, even at rush hour.

(Opposite) Port Authority Bus Terminal, Eighth Ave. at 40th St.

Mass-transportation terminals have always been thought of as the cities' ceremonial entranceways and, since they often provide the visitor with his first lasting impression of a city, it is fitting that they be designed with some grandeur. For all its marble tile and plastic foliage, however, this bus terminal does more to belittle the people who pass through it than to welcome them; and the unfortunate impersonality of its design is not dispelled by the decorations at Christmas time.

Luxor Baths, W. 46th St.

Around the turn of the century, public bathhouses were numerous and popular, serving as clubhouses for the masses who couldn't afford a private club. The Luxor, one of the handful that survive, is in the grand tradition; besides the pool and the massage room, its facilities include a dry-hot room, a pine steam room and an authentic Finnish sauna—all available every day to weary businessmen for a general admission fee of about $5.

(Opposite) Bryant Park.

A small but welcome breathing space in the heart of Manhattan, this was the site of New York's Crystal Palace, built in 1852 to house America's first World's Fair. In 1858, a disastrous fire destroyed the Crystal Palace within fifteen minutes. The pa:˙ was named for William Cullen Bryant in 1884; and is now the backyard of the New York Public Library at Fifth Ave. and 42nd St. Bryant Park provides a convenient location for city-sponsored cultural events, as for example the festivities in honor of Mexican Week, pictured here.

The Gotham Book Mart, 41 W. 47th St.

Frances Steloff, the former owner of the Book Mart, has for many years run the establishment in the tradition of Old World booksellers, intimately in-volved in the creation as well as the marketing of literary works. The roster of 20th-century writers associated with the Gotham is indeed impressive.

(Opposite) New York Public Library, 42nd St. and Fifth Ave.

The main reading-room of the library, designed by Carrère and Hastings, 1898-1911. Most of the mon-uments of Beaux-Arts architecture in New York have been either demolished or molested, but this masterpiece of the French style survives almost un-altered to remind us what a luxury a simple ampli-tude of space can be.

Looking south from 49th St. and Madison Ave.

The brightly illuminated building left center is the Union Carbide Building, 1960, Skidmore, Owings and Merrill. Behind it to the left is the Pan Am Building, 1963, Emery Roth and Sons, Pietro Bulleschi and Walter Gropius. At left, the Chemical Bank New York Trust Company, 1964, Emery Roth and Sons, is shown under construction. These are three of the latest and architecturally most distinguished entries in the real estate race which has recently turned Park Ave. into a curtain-walled canyon of glass.

(Opposite) Midtown, with RCA Building and Rockefeller Center.

In 1928, in an attempt to facilitate the relocation of the Metropolitan Opera Company, John D. Rockefeller took a lease on this property which made him personally responsible for a rental of $3,300,000 a year. He intended, of course, to sublease the land to the new opera house and to institutions which would want to build near it. The market crash of 1929, however, brought an end to the Met's plans, and Rockefeller, faced with the prospect of a staggering annual loss, decided to build an urban complex of his own. The happy result was Rockefeller Center, one of the best examples of comprehensive urban design in the world. At the lower left, the spires of St. Patrick's Cathedral, at Fifth Ave. and 51st St.

*(Opposite) Looking south on
Park Ave. from 55th St.*

It was the elegance of Park Ave. that made it a desirable corporate address in the first place. Today the atmosphere of elegance has almost completely vanished in the bustle of commercial activity on the avenue south of 59th St. One distinguished reminder of the Park Ave. that was is the Italian Renaissance four-story building at right, the Racquet and Tennis Club, built by McKim, Mead and White in 1918. Lever House, the first and perhaps the best of the glass-curtain-walled buildings, can be seen at the extreme right. It was built in 1952 by Skidmore, Owings and Merrill.

Coffee-break carts on Park Ave.

These little wagons provide a wry footnote to life in the technologically sophisticated Seventies. They are not used for street-vending; instead, at about 10 in the morning and 2:30 in the afternoon, hundreds of them are wheeled into the elevators of New York's gleaming glass skyscrapers to become instant snack bars on selected floors.

Park Ave. office girls.

Statistics may show that garment-making and printing are New York's two major industries, but everyone knows that offices are what the city is all about and that the clerk-typist—file clerk is the city's most important product.

Looking west from Sixth Ave. and 53rd St.

This photograph illustrates the remarkable rate of development of Sixth Ave. in the late Sixties. In the center is the recently completed New York Hilton Hotel. At left, the J. C. Penney Building is under construction. Just visible at the lower left is the construction activity on Saarinen's CBS Building. In the foreground center, the site of the new ABC Building has been cleared; while, to the right of the Hilton, on 54th St., is the old Ziegfeld Theater, since demolished to make way for the new corporate headquarters of Burlington Industries.

(Opposite) Midtown, late on a winter afternoon.

At the right, the Chrysler Building, 1930, William Van Alen, a superb example of Art Deco architecture. The gargoyles at the base of the chrome-steel spire are really and appropriately radiator caps.

The new architecture, midtown.
At left, the New York Hilton Hotel; at right, the Americana Hotel.

(Opposite) The Equitable Life Assurance Building and the Americana Hotel.

Eclecticism has always been a part of the charm of architecture in New York; and, over the years, the Manhattan skyline has been able to absorb the eccentricities of new styles with comparative ease. Lapidus's Americana (at right), built in 1962, with its glazed yellow and white brick and vast expanses of white marble facing, is New York's first and foremost example thus far of Floridian resort architecture.

55th St. Playhouse, 154 W. 55th St.

During the early Fifties, long before cinema became big business, the 55th St. Playhouse was one of the very few New York theaters which exhibited foreign "art" films.

(Opposite) The Ziegfeld Theater, 54th St. and Sixth Ave.

Until recently, this remarkable Art Deco building stood at 54th St., the last of the Broadway theaters to front on Sixth Ave. It was especially designed for Florenz Ziegfeld by Joseph Urban, set designer for the *Follies*, interior decorator and architect, who later played a key role in designing the Century of Progress Exposition in Chicago. The theater opened with the premiere performance of *Rio Rita* on Feb. 2, 1927.

Upper West Side, Broadway and 73rd St.

Upper West Side.

New York, unlike many European cities, has few places where people can sit and rest and, at the same time, remain close to the action. The fact that these ladies are willing to sit virtually in the middle of Broadway, surrounded by the noise and the dirt of city traffic, in order to keep an eye on the city's activity testifies to the need for pedestrian streets and plazas.

(Opposite) 82nd St., between Riverside Drive and West End Ave.

Manhattan's Upper West Side is a good deal less prestigious a place to live than a number of residential areas in other parts of the city. It is, however, a lively, fascinating area which offers much more diversity than some quieter neighborhoods. And, as this and the next few pictures show, some of its streets possess a charm quite unlike anything else to be seen in Manhattan.

349 W. 85th St.

84th St., between Riverside Drive and West End Ave.

Central Park.

The 840 acres which now comprise Central Park were acquired by a providentially far-sighted city administration in 1856 for $5,500,000. The next year, an open competition was held to determine the design of the projected park. The winning entry, a design called "Greensward," was submitted by Frederick Law Olmstead and Calvert Vaux. In spite of a number of 20th-century "improvements," the park remains largely as they intended it: a variety of differently landscaped areas make the most of the park's ample but limited size and provide opportunities for many activities without intimidating those who wish merely to stroll and relax. Here, an amateur photographer shooting ducks in the Pond.

(Opposite) Sunset at the Pond.

The Pond tucked into the southeastern corner of the park helps to isolate a sanctuary for migratory birds from the clamor of midtown Manhattan. The buildings shown here in the background flank 60th St. at Fifth Avenue.

The Wollman Memorial rink.

A relatively recent addition to the park's southeast corner, provides
facilities for skating in the winter and concerts in the summer. On
the other hand, it is a rather monumental violation of the park plan.
However attractive amenities such as this may appear, they ir-
revocably diminish the park's ability to provide the atmosphere of
unmolested landscape for which it was originally and successfully
designed.

Taking the sun in the park.
At the upper right, the Plaza Hotel, 1907, Henry J. Hardenbergh.

The Sheep Meadow.

The Central Park Sheep Meadow, shown here against a backdrop of midtown skyscrapers (Central Park South), is practically deserted in winter. In the summer it becomes the scene of concerts, demonstrations and festivals. The last open meadow in the park, it was named for the fact that sheep actually grazed here until 1934. The vintage lamppost is one of the 1907 series designed by Henry Bacon.

*Feeding time at the Seal Pond in the
Central Park Zoo.*

*In the Monkey House,
Central Park Zoo.*

Trefoil Arch, Central Park.

Olmstead's plans provided for almost complete separation of pedestrian and vehicular traffic so effectively that as one strolls under these decorative bridges one is scarcely aware that they were designed to eliminate intersections and traffic signals. Each of the bridges was individually designed by Calvert Vaux.

Harlem Meer, Central Park.

An altogether different illustration of separated traffic patterns at the northern end of the park, near 110th St.

The Conservatory Water.

Just off Fifth Ave. at 74th St., this pond was named for the conservatory planned for but never built on its eastern shore. Instead, it has become a center for model-boat enthusiasts.

Rowing on the Lake.
In the background, the towers of the San Remo
Apartments; 74th St. and Central Park West, 1930,
Emery Roth.

(Opposite) The Lake and the Terrace.

Designed by Vaux as the only formal architectural element of the Greensward plan. In the center, the Angel of the Waters atop the Bethesda Fountain. In 1966, in an effort to rehabilitate the flagging popularity of the Terrace, the city authorized the operation of the Fountain Cafe here. Its success has been spectacular. Sparked by the sprucing up of the Terrace, the Bethesda Fountain has become an impromptu gathering place for the younger and more colorful residents of the city. The floor show they provide and the magnificent scenery of the park itself, both free, make dining here one of the best summer bargains in New York.

A turn-of-the-century cast-iron gazebo on the west shore of Central Park Lake.

A detail of the elaborate stonework designed by
Jacob Wrey Mould for the Terrace.

In the background, the twin towers of the Majestic Apartments at
115 Central Park West. A fine example of Thirties elegance, they
were designed by the office of Irwin S. Chanin.

Fine arts in the park.

Conversation in the park.

127 E. 55th St.

At the end of the 19th century, the millionaires chose to build their mansions on upper Fifth Ave. and New York's very rich all decided to live on the Upper East Side. The area still has the greatest concentration of wealthy residents in Manhattan, and it remains a section of handsome townhouses and quiet elegance. Unfortunately, this lovely sphinx has moved on for parts unknown.

166. 32 E. 70th St.

Distinguished private homes of the late 19th and early 20th centuries line both sides of E. 70th St. from Third Ave. to Central Park. This one was designed by Taylor and Levy in 1910.

11 E. 68th St., between Fifth and Madison Aves.

Park Ave. at 70th St.

Ukrainian Institute of America, Fifth Ave. at 79th St.
This French Gothic château is the former Augustus van Horne
Stuyvesant House, and was designed by Stanford White.

133

East River Drive and the 59th St. Bridge.

Historically, New York has always been a harbor city. Today, its rivers remain commercially important, but they are no longer accessible to New Yorkers. In 1927, the city began to build its arterial highway system and, although these roads provide magnificent views to drivers, Battery Park is now the only place in Manhattan below 179th St. where the pedestrian can reach the water without consciously crossing this traffic barrier. In an age when large stretches of waterfront are wanted for recreational development, New York City finds that it has prematurely ceded its shoreline to the automobile.

(Opposite) The Solomon R. Guggenheim Museum, Fifth Ave. at 89th St.

This landmark of modern architecture is the only building in New York wholly designed by Frank Lloyd Wright, perhaps America's greatest architect. Constructed in 1959, it contains one of the greatest interiors in the world; unfortunately, however, the spiral design is not particularly suited to the exhibition of rectangular paintings.

Medicine man in Spanish East Harlem.

There are still sections of New York City where, for blocks at a stretch, there is nothing to contradict the impression that one has stumbled into some foreign city. Parts of the *barrio* are like this; all the signs and sounds are in Spanish.

Soda vendor, Spanish Harlem.

Spanish Harlem, card players.
The wall in the background supports the tracks of the Penn Central Railroad.

Dover Books on Art

200 DECORATIVE TITLE-PAGES, edited by A. Nesbitt. Fascinating and informative from a historical point of view, this beautiful collection of decorated titles will be a great inspiration to students of design, commercial artists, advertising designers, etc. A complete survey of the genre from the first known decorated title to work in the first decades of this century. Bibliography and sources of the plates. 222pp. 8⅜ x 11¼.

21264-5 Paperbound $3.50

ON THE LAWS OF JAPANESE PAINTING, H. P. Bowie. This classic work on the philosophy and technique of Japanese art is based on the author's first-hand experiences studying art in Japan. Every aspect of Japanese painting is described: the use of the brush and other materials; laws governing conception and execution; subjects for Japanese paintings, etc. The best possible substitute for a series of lessons from a great Oriental master. Index. xv + 117pp. + 66 plates. 6⅛ x 9¼.

20030-2 Paperbound $2.50

A HANDBOOK OF ANATOMY FOR ART STUDENTS, Arthur Thomson. This long-popular text teaches any student, regardless of level of technical competence, all the subtleties of human anatomy. Clear photographs, numerous line sketches and diagrams of bones, joints, etc. Use it as a text for home study, as a supplement to life class work, or as a lifelong sourcebook and reference volume. Author's prefaces. 67 plates, containing 40 line drawings, 86 photographs—mostly full page. 211 figures. Appendix. Index. xx + 459pp. 5⅜ x 8⅜. 21163-0 Paperbound $3.50

WHITTLING AND WOODCARVING, E. J. Tangerman. With this book, a beginner who is moderately handy can whittle or carve scores of useful objects, toys for children, gifts, or simply pass hours creatively and enjoyably. "Easy as well as instructive reading," N. Y. Herald Tribune Books. 464 illustrations, with appendix and index. x + 293pp. 5½ x 8⅛.

20965-2 Paperbound $2.00

ONE HUNDRED AND ONE PATCHWORK PATTERNS, Ruby Short McKim. Whether you have made a hundred quilts or none at all, you will find this the single most useful book on quiltmaking. There are 101 full patterns (all exact size) with full instructions for cutting and sewing. In addition there is some really choice folklore about the origin of the ingenious pattern names: "Monkey Wrench," "Road to California," "Drunkard's Path," "Crossed Canoes," to name a few. Over 500 illustrations. 124 pp. 7⅞ x 10¾. 20773-0 Paperbound $2.00

ART AND GEOMETRY, W. M. Ivins, Jr. Challenges the idea that the foundations of modern thought were laid in ancient Greece. Pitting Greek tactile-muscular intuitions of space against modern visual intuitions, the author, for 30 years curator of prints, Metropolitan Museum of Art, analyzes the differences between ancient and Renaissance painting and sculpture and tells of the first fruitful investigations of perspective. x + 113pp. 5⅜ x 8⅜. 20941-5 Paperbound $1.50

AN ATLAS OF ANIMAL ANATOMY FOR ARTISTS, W. Ellenberger, H. Baum, H. Dittrich. The largest, richest animal anatomy for artists in English. Form, musculature, tendons, bone structure, expression, detailed cross sections of head, other features, of the horse, lion, dog, cat, deer, seal, kangaroo, cow, bull, goat, monkey, hare, many other animals. "Highly recommended," DESIGN. Second, revised, enlarged edition with new plates from Cuvier, Stubbs, etc. 288 illustrations. 153pp. 11⅜ x 9.

20082-5 Paperbound $3.00

ANIMAL DRAWING: ANATOMY AND ACTION FOR ARTISTS, C. R. Knight. 158 studies, with full accompanying text, of such animals as the gorilla, bear, bison, dromedary, camel, vulture, pelican, iguana, shark, etc., by one of the greatest modern masters of animal drawing. Innumerable tips on how to get life expression into your work. "An excellent reference work," SAN FRANCISCO CHRONICLE. 158 illustrations. 156pp. 10½ x 8½.

20426-X Paperbound $3.00

ARCHITECTURAL AND PERSPECTIVE DESIGNS, Giuseppe Galli Bibiena. 50 imaginative scenic drawings of Giuseppe Galli Bibiena, principal theatrical engineer and architect to the Viennese court of Charles VI. Aside from its interest to art historians, students, and art lovers, there is a whole Baroque world of material in this book for the commercial artist. Portrait of Charles VI by Martin de Meytens. 1 allegorical plate. 50 additional plates. New introduction. vi + 103pp. 10⅛ x 13¼.

21263-7 Paperbound $2.50

HANDBOOK OF DESIGNS AND DEVICES, C. P. Hornung. A remarkable working collection of 1836 basic designs and variations, all copyright-free. Variations of circle, line, cross, diamond, swastika, star, scroll, shield, many more. Notes on symbolism. "A necessity to every designer who would be original without having to labor heavily," ARTIST AND ADVERTISER. 204 plates. 240pp. 5⅜ x 8. 20125-2 Paperbound $2.00

CHINESE HOUSEHOLD FURNITURE, G. N. Kates. A summary of virtually everything that is known about authentic Chinese furniture before it was contaminated by the influence of the West. The text covers history of styles, materials used, principles of design and craftsmanship, and furniture arrangement—all fully illustrated. xiii + 190pp. 5⅝ x 8½.

20958-X Paperbound $2.00

DECORATIVE ART OF THE SOUTHWESTERN INDIANS, D. S. Sides. 300 black and white reproductions from one of the most beautiful art traditions of the primitive world, ranging from the geometric art of the Great Pueblo period of the 13th century to modern folk art. Motives from basketry, beadwork, Zuni masks, Hopi kachina dolls, Navajo sand pictures and blankets, and ceramic ware. Unusual and imaginative designs will inspire craftsmen in all media, and commercial artists may reproduce any of them without permission or payment. xviii + 101pp. 5⅝ x 8⅜. 20139-2 Paperbound $1.50

PINE FURNITURE OF EARLY NEW ENGLAND, R. H. Kettell. Over 400 illustrations, over 50 working drawings of early New England chairs, benches, beds, cupboards, mirrors, shelves, tables, other furniture esteemed for simple beauty and character. "Rich store of illustrations . . . emphasizes the individuality and varied design," ANTIQUES. 413 illustrations, 55 working drawings. 475pp. 8 x 10¾. 20145-7 Clothbound $10.00

BASIC BOOKBINDING, A. W. Lewis. Enables both beginners and experts to rebind old books or bind paperbacks in hard covers. Treats materials, tools; gives step-by-step instruction in how to collate a book, sew it, back it, make boards, etc. 261 illus. Appendices. 155pp. 5⅜ x 8. 20169-4 Paperbound $1.75

DESIGN MOTIFS OF ANCIENT MEXICO, J. Enciso. Nearly 90% of these 766 superb designs from Aztec, Olmec, Totonac, Maya, and Toltec origins are unobtainable elsewhere. Contains plumed serpents, wind gods, animals, demons, dancers, monsters, etc. Excellent applied design source. Originally $17.50. 766 illustrations, thousands of motifs. 192pp. 6⅛ x 9¼. 20084-1 Paperbound $2.50

A DIDEROT PICTORIAL ENCYCLOPEDIA OF TRADES AND INDUSTRY. Manufacturing and the Technical Arts in Plates Selected from "L'Encyclopédie ou Dictionnaire Raisonné des Sciences, des Arts, et des Métiers," of Denis Diderot, edited with text by C. Gillispie. Over 2000 illustrations on 485 full-page plates. Magnificent 18th-century engravings of men, women, and children working at such trades as milling flour, cheesemaking, charcoal burning, mining, silverplating, shoeing horses, making fine glass, printing, hundreds more, showing details of machinery, different steps in sequence, etc. A remarkable art work, but also the largest collection of working figures in print, copyright-free, for art directors, designers, etc. Two vols. 920pp. 9 x 12. Heavy library cloth. 22284-5, 22283-3 Two volume set $27.50

SILK SCREEN TECHNIQUES, J. Biegeleisen, M. Cohn. A practical step-by-step home course in one of the most versatile, least expensive graphic arts processes. How to build an inexpensive silk screen, prepare stencils, print, achieve special textures, use color, etc. Every step explained, diagrammed. 149 illustrations, 201pp. 6⅛ x 9¼. 20433-2 Paperbound $2.00

STICKS AND STONES, Lewis Mumford. An examination of forces influencing American architecture: the medieval tradition in early New England, the classical influence in Jefferson's time, the Brown Decades, the imperial facade, the machine age, etc. "A truly remarkable book," SAT. REV. OF LITERATURE. 2nd revised edition. 21 illus. xvii + 240pp. 5⅜ x 8. 20202-X Paperbound $2.00

THE AUTOBIOGRAPHY OF AN IDEA, Louis Sullivan. The architect whom Frank Lloyd Wright called "the master," records the development of the theories that revolutionized America's skyline. 34 full-page plates of Sullivan's finest work. New introduction by R. M. Line. xiv + 335pp. 5⅜ x 8. 20281-X Paperbound $2.50

ANIMALS IN MOTION, Eadweard Muybridge. The largest collection of animal action photos in print. 34 different animals (horses, mules, oxen, goats, camels, pigs, cats, lions, gnus, deer, monkeys, eagles—and 22 others) in 132 characteristic actions. All 3919 photographs are taken in series at speeds up to 1/1600th of a second, offering artists, biologists, cartoonists a remarkable opportunity to see exactly how an ostrich's head bobs when running, how a lion puts his foot down, how an elephant's knee bends, how a bird flaps his wings, thousands of other hard-to-catch details. "A really marvellous series of plates," NATURE. 380 full-page plates. Heavy glossy stock, reinforced binding with headbands. 7⅞ x 10¾.   20203-8 Clothbound $12.50

THE BOOK OF SIGNS, R. Koch. 493 symbols—crosses, monograms, astrological, biological symbols, runes, etc.—from ancient manuscripts, cathedrals, coins, catacombs, pottery. May be reproduced permission-free. 493 illustrations by Fritz Kredel. 104pp. 6⅛ x 9¼.   20162-7 Paperbound $1.25

A HANDBOOK OF EARLY ADVERTISING ART, C. P. Hornung. The largest collection of copyright-free early advertising art ever compiled. Vol. I: 2,000 illustrations of animals, old automobiles, buildings, allegorical figures, fire engines, Indians, ships, trains, more than 33 other categories! Vol. II: Over 4,000 typographical specimens; 600 Roman, Gothic, Barnum, Old English faces; 630 ornamental type faces; hundreds of scrolls, initials, flourishes, etc. "A remarkable collection," PRINTERS' INK.

Vol. I: Pictorial Volume. Over 2000 illustrations. 256pp. 9 x 12.
                20122-8 Clothbound $12.50

Vol. II: Typographical Volume. Over 4000 specimens. 319pp. 9 x 12.   20123-6 Clothbound $12.50

Two volume set, Clothbound, only $25.00

THE UNIVERSAL PENMAN, George Bickham. Exact reproduction of beautiful 18th-century book of handwriting. 22 complete alphabets in finest English roundhand, other scripts, over 2000 elaborate flourishes, 122 calligraphic illustrations, etc. Material is copyright-free. "An essential part of any art library, and a book of permanent value," AMERICAN ARTIST. 212 plates. 224pp. 9 x 13¾.   20020-5 Clothbound $12.50

AN ATLAS OF ANATOMY FOR ARTISTS, F. Schider. This standard work contains 189 full-page plates, more than 647 illustrations of all aspects of the human skeleton, musculature, cutaway portions of the body, each part of the anatomy, hand forms, eyelids, breasts, location of muscles under the flesh, etc. 59 plates illustrate how Michelangelo, da Vinci, Goya, 15 others, drew human anatomy. New 3rd edition enlarged by 52 new illustrations by Cloquet, Barcsay. "The standard reference tool," AMERICAN LIBRARY ASSOCIATION. "Excellent," AMERICAN ARTIST. 189 plates, 647 illustrations. xxvi + 192pp. 7⅞ x 10⅝.   20241-0 Clothbound $6.50

GREEK REVIVAL ARCHITECTURE IN AMERICA, T. Hamlin. A comprehensive study of the American Classical Revival, its regional variations, reasons for its success and eventual decline. Profusely illustrated with photos, sketches, floor plans and sections, displaying the work of almost every important architect of the time. 2 appendices. 39 figures, 94 plates containing 221 photos, 62 architectural designs, drawings, etc. 324-item classified bibliography. Index. xi + 439pp. 5⅜ x 8½.

21148-7   Paperbound $3.50

CREATIVE LITHOGRAPHY AND HOW TO DO IT, Grant Arnold. Written by a man who practiced and taught lithography for many years, this highly useful volume explains all the steps of the lithographic process from tracing the drawings on the stone to printing the lithograph, with helpful hints for solving special problems. Index. 16 reproductions of lithographs. 11 drawings. xv + 214pp. of text. 5⅜ x 8½.

21208-4   Paperbound $2.25

TEACH YOURSELF ANTIQUE COLLECTING, E. Bradford. An excellent, brief guide to collecting British furniture, silver, pictures and prints, pewter, pottery and porcelain, Victoriana, enamels, clocks or other antiques. Much background information difficult to find elsewhere. 15pp. of illus. 215pp. 7 x 4¼.

21368-4   Clothbound $2.00

PAINTING IN THE FAR EAST, L. Binyon. A study of over 1500 years of Oriental art by one of the world's outstanding authorities. The author chooses the most important masters in each period—Wu Tao-tzu, Toba Sojo, Kanaoka, Li Lung-mien, Masanobu, Okio, etc.—and examines the works, schools, and influence of each within their cultural context. 42 photographs. Sources of original works and selected bibliography. Notes including list of principal painters by periods. xx + 297pp. 6⅛ x 9¼.

20520-7   Paperbound $2.50

THE ALPHABET AND ELEMENTS OF LETTERING, F. W. Goudy. A beautifully illustrated volume on the aesthetics of letters and type faces and their history and development. Each plate consists of 15 forms of a single letter with the last plate devoted to the ampersand and the numerals. "A sound guide for all persons engaged in printing or drawing," Saturday Review. 27 full-page plates. 48 additional figures. xii + 131pp. 7⅞ x 10¾.

20792-7   Paperbound $2.25

THE COMPLETE BOOK OF SILK SCREEN PRINTING PRODUCTION, J. I. Biegeleisen. Here is a clear and complete picture of every aspect of silk screen technique and press operation—from individually operated manual presses to modern automatic ones. Unsurpassed as a guidebook for setting up shop, making shop operation more efficient, finding out about latest methods and equipment; or as a textbook for use in teaching, studying, or learning all aspects of the profession. 124 figures. Index. Bibliography. List of Supply Sources. xi + 253pp. 5⅜ x 8½.

21100-2   Paperbound $2.75

MASTERPIECES OF FURNITURE, Verna Cook Salomonsky.
Photographs and measured drawings of some of the finest examples of Colonial American, 17th century English, Windsor,
Sheraton, Hepplewhite, Chippendale, Louis XIV, Queen Anne,
and various other furniture styles. The textual matter includes
information on traditions, characteristics, background, etc. of
various pieces. 101 plates. Bibliography. 224pp. 7⅞ x 10¾.

21381-1 Paperbound $3.00

PRIMITIVE ART, Franz Boas. In this exhaustive volume, a
great American anthropologist analyzes all the fundamental
traits of primitive art, covering the formal element in art, repre-
sentative art, symbolism, style, literature, music, and the dance.
Illustrations of Indian embroidery, paleolithic paintings, woven
blankets, wing and tail designs, totem poles, cutlery, earthen-
ware, baskets and many other primitive objects and motifs. Over
900 illustrations. 376pp. 5⅜ x 8.   20025-6 Paperbound $2.50

*AN INTRODUCTION TO A HISTORY OF WOODCUT, A. M.
Hind.* Nearly all of this authoritative 2-volume set is devoted to
the 15th century—the period during which the woodcut came of
age as an important art form. It is the most complete compendium
of information on this period, the artists who contributed to it,
and their technical and artistic accomplishments. Profusely illustrated with cuts by 15th century masters, and later works
for comparative purposes. 484 illustrations. 5 indexes. Total of
xi + 838pp. 5⅜ x 8½. Two-vols. 20952-0, 20953-0 Paperbound $7.50

A HISTORY OF ENGRAVING AND ETCHING, A. M. Hind.
Beginning with the anonymous masters of 15th century engraving, this highly regarded and thorough survey carries you
through Italy, Holland, and Germany to the great engravers and
beginnings of etching in the 16th century, through the portrait
engravers, master etchers, practicioners of mezzotint, crayon
manner and stipple, aquatint, color prints, to modern etching
in the period just prior to World War I. Beautifully illustrated
—sharp clear prints on heavy opaque paper. Author's preface.
3 appendixes. 111 illustrations. xviii + 487 pp. 5⅜ x 8½.

20954-7 Paperbound $3.50

ART STUDENTS' ANATOMY, E. J. Farris. Teaching anatomy
by using chiefly living objects for illustration, this study has
enjoyed long popularity and success in art courses and home-
study programs. All the basic elements of the human anatomy
are illustrated in minute detail, diagrammed and pictured as they
pass through common movements and actions. 158 drawings,
photographs, and roentgenograms. Glossary of anatomical terms.
x + 159pp. 5⅝ x 8⅜.   20744-7 Paperbound $1.50

COLONIAL LIGHTING, A. H. Hayward. The only book to cover
the fascinating story of lamps and other lighting devices in
America. Beginning with rush light holders used by the early
settlers, it ranges through the elaborate chandeliers of the Federal period, illustrating 647 lamps. Of great value to antique
collectors, designers, and historians of arts and crafts. Revised
and enlarged by James R. Marsh. xxxi + 198pp. 5⅝ x 8¼.

20975-X Paperbound $2.50

ART ANATOMY, Dr. William Rimmer. One of the few books on art anatomy that are themselves works of art, this is a faithful reproduction (rearranged for handy use) of the extremely rare masterpiece of the famous 19th century anatomist, sculptor, and art teacher. Beautiful, clear line drawings show every part of the body—bony structure, muscles, features, etc. Unusual are the sections on falling bodies, foreshortenings, muscles in tension, grotesque personalities, and Rimmer's remarkable interpretation of emotions and personalities as expressed by facial features. It will supplement every other book on art anatomy you are likely to have. Reproduced clearer than the lithographic original (which sells for $500 on up on the rare book market.) Over 1,200 illustrations. xiii + 153pp. 7¾ x 10¾.
20908-3 Paperbound $2.50

THE CRAFTSMAN'S HANDBOOK, Cennino Cennini. The finest English translation of IL LIBRO DELL' ARTE, the 15th century introduction to art technique that is both a mirror of Quatrocento life and a source of many useful but nearly forgotten facets of the painter's art. 4 illustrations. xxvii + 142pp. D. V. Thompson, translator. 5⅜ x 8.   20054-X Paperbound $2.00

THE BROWN DECADES, Lewis Mumford. A picture of the "buried renaissance" of the post-Civil War period, and the founding of modern architecture (Sullivan, Richardson, Root, Roebling), landscape development (Marsh, Olmstead, Eliot), and the graphic arts (Homer, Eakins, Ryder). 2nd revised, enlarged edition. Bibliography. 12 illustrations. xiv + 266 pp. 5⅜ x 8.
20200-3 Paperbound $2.00

THE STYLES OF ORNAMENT, A. Speltz. The largest collection of line ornament in print, with 3750 numbered illustrations arranged chronologically from Egypt, Assyria, Greeks, Romans, Etruscans, through Medieval, Renaissance, 18th century, and Victorian. No permissions, no fees needed to use or reproduce illustrations. 400 plates with 3750 illustrations. Bibliography. Index. 640pp. 6 x 9.   20577-6 Paperbound $3.75

THE ART OF ETCHING, E. S. Lumsden. Every step of the etching process from essential materials to completed proof is carefully and clearly explained, with 24 annotated plates exemplifying every technique and approach discussed. The book also features a rich survey of the art, with 105 annotated plates by masters. Invaluable for beginner to advanced etcher. 374pp. 5⅜ x 8.   20049-3 Paperbound $3.00

OF THE JUST SHAPING OF LETTERS, Albrecht Dürer. This remarkable volume reveals Albrecht Dürer's rules for the geometric construction of Roman capitals and the formation of Gothic lower case and capital letters, complete with construction diagrams and directions. Of considerable practical interest to the contemporary illustrator, artist, and designer. Translated from the Latin text of the edition of 1535 by R. T. Nichol. Numerous letterform designs, construction diagrams, illustrations. iv + 43pp. 7⅞ x 10¾.   21306-4 Paperbound $2.00

PRINCIPLES OF ART HISTORY, H. Wölfflin. This remarkably instructive work demonstrates the tremendous change in artistic conception from the 14th to the 18th centuries, by analyzing 164 works by Botticelli, Dürer, Hobbema, Holbein, Hals, Titian, Rembrandt, Vermeer, etc., and pointing out exactly what is meant by "baroque," "classic," "primitive," "picturesque," and other basic terms of art history and criticism. "A remarkable lesson in the art of seeing," SAT. REV. OF LITERATURE. Translated from the 7th German edition. 150 illus. 254pp. 6⅛ x 9¼.   20276-3 Paperbound $2.50

FOUNDATIONS OF MODERN ART, A. Ozenfant. Stimulating discussion of human creativity from paleolithic cave painting to modern painting, architecture, decorative arts. Fully illustrated with works of Gris, Lipchitz, Léger, Picasso, primitive, modern artifacts, architecture, industrial art, much more. 226 illustrations. 368pp. 6⅛ x 9¼.   20215-1 Paperbound $3.00

METALWORK AND ENAMELLING, H. Maryon. Probably the best book ever written on the subject. Tells everything necessary for the home manufacture of jewelry, rings, ear pendants, bowls, etc. Covers materials, tools, soldering, filigree, setting stones, raising patterns, repoussé work, damascening, niello, cloisonné, polishing, assaying, casting, and dozens of other techniques. The best substitute for apprenticeship to a master metal-worker. 363 photos and figures. 374pp. 5½ x 8½.
                    22702-2 Paperbound $3.50

SHAKER FURNITURE, E. D. and F. Andrews. The most illuminating study of Shaker furniture ever written. Covers chronology, craftsmanship, houses, shops, etc. Includes over 200 photographs of chairs, tables, clocks, beds, benches, etc. "Mr. & Mrs. Andrews know all there is to know about Shaker furniture," Mark Van Doren, NATION. 48 full-page plates. 192pp. 7⅞ x 10¾.   20679-3 Paperbound $2.75

LETTERING AND ALPHABETS, J. A. Cavanagh. An unabridged reissue of "Lettering," containing the full discussion, analysis, illustration of 89 basic hand lettering styles based on Caslon, Bodoni, Gothic, many other types. Hundreds of technical hints on construction, strokes, pens, brushes, etc. 89 alphabets, 72 lettered specimens, which may be reproduced permission-free. 121pp. 9¾ x 8.   20053-1 Paperbound $1.50

THE HUMAN FIGURE IN MOTION, Eadweard Muybridge. The largest collection in print of Muybridge's famous high-speed action photos. 4789 photographs in more than 500 action-strip-sequences (at shutter speeds up to 1/6000th of a second) illustrate men, women, children—mostly undraped—performing such actions as walking, running, getting up, lying down, carrying objects, throwing, etc. "An unparalleled dictionary of action for all artists," AMERICAN ARTIST. 390 full-page plates, with 4789 photographs. Heavy glossy stock, reinforced binding with headbands. 7⅞ x 10¾.   20204-6 Clothbound $12.50

AFRICAN SCULPTURE, Ladislas Segy. 163 full-page plates illustrating masks, fertility figures, ceremonial objects, etc., of 50 West and Central African tribes—95% never before illustrated. 34-page introduction to African sculpture. "Mr. Segy is one of its top authorities," NEW YORKER. 164 full-page photographic plates. Introduction. Bibliography. 244pp. 6⅛ x 9¼.

20396-4 Paperbound $2.25

CALLIGRAPHY, J. G. Schwandner. First reprinting in 200 years of this legendary book of beautiful handwriting. Over 300 ornamental initials, 12 complete calligraphic alphabets, over 150 ornate frames and panels, 75 calligraphic pictures of cherubs, stags, lions, etc., thousands of flourishes, scrolls, etc., by the greatest 18th-century masters. All material can be copied or adapted without permission. Historical introduction. 158 full-page plates. 368pp. 9 x 13.   20475-8 Clothbound $10.00

PRINTED EPHEMERA, edited and collected by John Lewis. This book contains centuries of design, typographical and pictorial motives in proven, effective commercial layouts. Hundreds of the most striking examples of labels, tickets, posters, wrappers, programs, menus, and other items have been collected in this handsome and useful volume, along with information on the dimensions and colors of the original, printing processes used, stylistic notes on typography and design, etc. Study this book and see how the best commercial artists of the past and present have solved their particular problems. Most of the material is copyright free. 713 illustrations, many in color. Illustrated index of type faces included. Glossary of technical terms. Indexes. 288pp. 9¼ x 12.   22284-5, 22285-3 Clothbound $15.00

DESIGN FOR ARTISTS AND CRAFTSMEN, Louis Wolchonok. Recommended for either individual or classroom use, this book helps you to create original designs from things about you, from geometric patterns, from plants, animals, birds, humans, landscapes, manmade objects. "A great contribution," N. Y. Society of Craftsmen. 113 exercises with hints and diagrams. More than 1280 illustrations. xv + 207pp. 7⅞ x 10¾.

20274-7 Paperbound $2.75

HANDBOOK OF ORNAMENT, F. S. Meyer. One of the largest collections of copyright-free traditional art: over 3300 line cuts of Greek, Roman, Medieval, Renaissance, Baroque, 18th and 19th century art motifs (tracery, geometric elements, flower and animal motifs, etc.) and decorated objects (chairs, thrones, weapons, vases, jewelry, armor, etc.). Full text. 300 plates. 3300 illustrations. 562pp. 5⅜ x 8.   20302-6 Paperbound $2.75

THREE CLASSICS OF ITALIAN CALLIGRAPHY, Oscar Ogg, ed. Exact reproductions of three famous Renaissance calligraphic works: Arrighi's OPERINA and IL MODO, Tagliente's LO PRESENTE LIBRO, and Palatino's LIBRO NUOVO. More than 200 complete alphabets, thousands of lettered specimens, in Papal Chancery and other beautiful, ornate handwriting. Introduction. 245 plates. 282pp. 6⅛ x 9¼.   20212-7 Paperbound $2.75

LANDSCAPE GARDENING IN JAPAN, Josiah Conder. A detailed picture of Japanese gardening techniques and ideas, the artistic principles incorporated in the Japanese garden, and the religious and ethical concepts at the heart of those principles. Preface. 92 illustrations, plus all 40 full-page plates from the Supplement. Index. xv + 299pp. 8⅜ x 11¼.

21216-5 Paperbound $3.50

DESIGN AND FIGURE CARVING, E. J. Tangerman. "Anyone who can peel a potato can carve," states the author, and in this unusual book he shows you how, covering every stage in detail from very simple exercises working up to museum-quality pieces. Terrific aid for hobbyists, arts and crafts counselors, teachers, those who wish to make reproductions for the commercial market. Appendix: How to Enlarge a Design. Brief bibliography. Index. 1298 figures. x + 289pp. 5⅜ x 8½.

21209-2 Paperbound $2.00

THE STANDARD BOOK OF QUILT MAKING AND COLLECTING, M. Ickis. Even if you are a beginner, you will soon find yourself quilting like an expert, by following these clearly drawn patterns, photographs, and step-by-step instructions. Learn how to plan the quilt, to select the pattern to harmonize with the design and color of the room, to choose materials. Over 40 full-size patterns. Index. 483 illustrations. One color plate. xi + 276pp. 6¾ x 9½.   20582-7 Paperbound $2.50

LOST EXAMPLES OF COLONIAL ARCHITECTURE, J. M. Howells. This book offers a unique guided tour through America's architectural past, all of which is either no longer in existence or so changed that its original beauty has been destroyed. More than 275 clear photos of old churches, dwelling houses, public buildings, business structures, etc. 245 plates, containing 281 photos and 9 drawings, floorplans, etc. New Index. xvii + 248pp. 7⅞ x 10¾.   21143-6 Paperbound $3.00

A HISTORY OF COSTUME, Carl Köhler. The most reliable and authentic account of the development of dress from ancient times through the 19th century. Based on actual pieces of clothing that have survived, using paintings, statues and other reproductions only where originals no longer exist. Hundreds of illustrations, including detailed patterns for many articles. Highly useful for theatre and movie directors, fashion designers, illustrators, teachers. Edited and augmented by Emma von Sichart. Translated by Alexander K. Dallas. 594 illustrations. 464pp. 5⅛ x 7⅛.

21030-8 Paperbound $3.00

Dover publishes books on commercial art, art history, crafts, design, art classics; also books on music, literature, science, mathematics, puzzles and entertainments, chess, engineering, biology, philosophy, psychology, languages, history, and other fields. For free circulars write to Dept. DA, Dover Publications, Inc., 180 Varick St., New York, N.Y. 10014.